A DIFFERENT DRUMMER

BY THE SAME AUTHOR

A DIFFERENT DRUMMER

JACK CLEMO

TABB HOUSE
Padstow, Cornwall

First published in Great Britain 1986
Tabb House, 11 Church Street, Padstow, Cornwall, PL28 8BG

ISBN 0   907018   53   X

A grant by South West Arts towards the publication of this
book is gratefully acknowledged.

WITH THE ASSISTANCE OF

SOUTH WEST ARTS

Printed by Quintrell & Co. Ltd., Trenant Industrial Estate,
Egloshayle, Wadebridge, Cornwall, PL27 6HB.

IN TRIBUTE TO
MY MOTHER

ACKNOWLEDGMENTS

My thanks are due to the editors of the following periodicals in which many of these poems have been published: *Anglo-Welsh Review*, *Christian Woman*, *Cornish Banner*, *Dorset Year Book*, *Journal of Indian Writing in English*, *Meridian*, *New Poetry*, *Outposts*, *Pennine Platform*, *PN Review*, *Powys Review*, *Resurg-ence*, *South-west Review* and *Third Way*. 'Coppice Tarn' was broadcast in a BBC 'Westward Look' radio programme. 'The Restored See' was printed in a souvenir pamphlet issued to mark the centenary of the Truro Anglican diocese in 1977. 'Bethel' appeared in a similar pamphlet commemorating the centenary of Trethosa chapel in 1976, and was reprinted in the *Methodist Conference Handbook* for 1982.

Material for the poem on Jim Elliot was drawn from his letters and diaries, published posthumously in *Shadow of the Almighty*, by Elisabeth Elliot, to whom I am indebted for her approval of the poem. The two poems on Catholic visionaries were based on episodes described in *A Woman Clothed With The Sun*, edited by John Delaney.

CONTENTS

VISTAS WITHIN MARRIAGE

What is stored in the clasping moment?
Meal and map for the shared journey.
Here we reform our tastes, unitedly
Choose a land, explore what blazed and blent
In the love-touch. Before the clasping
Each of us spun, a world apart,
Giddy with hunger and groping. Now we start
On a firm cosmos, melt the flat self's wavering
In ribbed and racing truth: entwined
Minds and hearts clear the resigned
Riddle of personality.

The puzzling rays broke on false mirrors
While our lives swung in solitary frost:
Mine a pent, worked-out valley - clots of mossed
Crumbling concrete near a brook, clawed by furze,
Bramble, nettle, where once a water-wheel
Spun giddily till a stone-mill stopped.
Your world knew palm-shade, but the sand
    swayed, dropped
In a slick slant seaward. We lost the old ideal -
My pounding knuckled iron and flange-flash,
Your straight-backed frost-defying palms. Fusion
    must smash
Mocking mirrors, show substance we can trust.

A DIFFERENT DRUMMER

'If a man does not keep instep with his fellows,
it may be because he hears a different drummer'. — Thoreau

Just after dawn the foreign sound
Starts the pilgrim off on the wrong foot,
Tramping his lonely inner slum,
His soul's Samaria, spellbound
By the rhythm of the well-head drum
Calling from the desert in an unknown tongue:
'Tell the harlot there's living water . . .'
He sees, through tears, the casual young
Stepping to the rhythm of balls bouncing,
Tent-pegs hammered, the cold announcing
Voices of teachers. The clash grows hotter.

Mystic forenoon is all in dirge motion,
Slow burdened pace of his starved nature
As he learns the strange drum-tap, yearns to explore
A penitent way to cleansed passion,
But finds no partner. If rains pour,
Feeding the well, their beat is grief-wrung:
'Tell the virtuous there's new wine . . .'
He sees, through tears, the decent young
Stepping to the gay tempo, the unpricked
Sway of custom, while he, in conflict,
Heeds only Samaria's throbbing sign.

One with the tired God and the burning blood
Of the woman parched for worship, he treads
In blind faith his love-measure, seeming a loss
To the world's swing, proud or subdued.
Drums of Mammon, Mars and Demos,
Jungle tom-toms, batter his fierce drilled song:
'Tell all there's a sacrament . . .'
How does the misfit end? Is the young
Self-exile a waste? No, not this type.
Samaria makes reverence more subtly ripe,
Makes the shared dance at sunset - mine now
    - more vibrant.

UNEARTHED

Sunset on St Valentine's day
Revealed something odd: an abrupt gasp,
Not due to frosty air, made us halt on the flat road
That sneaked under prickly sleeves from the stone-pits.

For weeks past the trundling transport lorries
Had jarred our walls as we woke in the eighth year
Of our creed-bedded marriage. They had fussed and
    snorted
Through day-long gales and rain, removing
From behind the engine-house a low dump
Which had first fingered, then crushed and buried
One of my grandfather's lean farm fields.

An excavator's bucket may have swung too deep
At the old grass level: what it unearthed
Was the object that startled us, forcing
Austere incongruities on our Valentine mood.

The skull and bones of a horse lay exposed
In the thinking red wash from a dry sky.
The white fractured frame gleamed amid mud and
    bush-tufts,
Placid and tacit, transmitting
A sharp, aged cacophony to our rounded key.

But it was one of those moments – I have had many –
When faith is known by a past catharsis
That purged the soul of negative awe, the false
      reverence
For tragic ends, the sense of an ultimate
In the earth's clutch at our worn-out clothing.

Beyond the brief bustle, the surface speculation,
The healthy picture of a cart in the farmyard,
My grandfather singing as he took the reins –
Beyond this, nothing entered or disturbed
The poet's storehouse of relevant symbols.
They were creative and redemptive only, to be shared
With the partner who had trustfully come with me
Out into the crisp and fearless evening light.

A TASTE OF SCILLY

Not all hermit-waste, not all a scowl of mine-stacks
Those unbandaged youth years: my optic sense, alert
For contour and colour, was not crabbed
Wholly by the industrial blotch,
Spidery web of tip-wires, catapulted boulders
Slowed in the slither of quartz-grains down the dump's
      slope.

Soft loveliness also fed the artist
With the normal poignant gleam, the time-stilling smile.
On a pitching deck, bound for the Scillies,
I plumbed the mature pang of exile,
Watching Land's End break contact, leave me like Ulysses,
Voyaging in an infinite coil of waters
With a hint of fabled treasure in the small scars
Out there on the grey-blue skyline,
Shaping solid as the ship plunged ahead.

The noon-stripped archipelago
Came alive with unbearable pathos:
Fragile shelves of the earth's crust upthrust,
Trustful enough for copulation and church bells,
Trustful in the puffins' nesting instinct
And the planted bulbs' bought carnival of lilies . . .
Something was added to me there
Which you must note when I speak of solitude.

I remember the tea-room on Hugh Town pier –
Wide windows open, sea-breeze from tropical Tresco
Fretting among tables, trippers, jangled women
Shrill with a tired dusty glamour,
Mainland hair-styles and neuroses.
The breeze seemed to play more soothingly,
The sunshafts pulse more gently, on the island girls –
Efficient waitresses, yet powerfully apart,
Their mermaid hair loose, tossed over their backs,
Their faces stark, moulded by remote tidal mystery.
I sensed the depth, the peace, the invincible isolation –
Perhaps defensive, akin to mine:
The invading values rang false to them and me.

I had just tramped back from Peninnis,
Where I viewed the lighthouse – a pale stumpy tower
Passive in a broken cradle of crags,
Awaiting its hour of service:
Darkness and the louder Atlantic pounding,
The puffins at rest on Annet,
The blind brows of Samson wet in starshine,
The last bedroom lamps out, the bare trust undisturbed.

POEM AT SIXTY

So many poets, before they reached three-score,
Let their despair employ a coroner.
As the March rain now hammers
The slate above my birth-room, I recall a few:
Chatterton, Beddoes, Davidson, Mew,
Hart Crane, Vachel Lindsay . . . I think my stars
Were as tragic as theirs, yet my pen
Still throws up clues to my survival,
A massed chorus with no broken bars.

The hill-setting has changed wickedly for the worse:
The daily slobber of spawned crystals
Creeps nearer my windows, blocking the view
Of grassy dome, wood and pasture
Which in infancy I watched with vague wonder,
And in youth with glum indifference
As my inner life submerged, feeling the scabs of the
        outcast
More true than the comforting green.

Lorry-tracks and footpaths have multiplied
Around the marooned home walls,
Twisting past sheds, dumps, mica-beds,
Where cows grazed when I took my first stride
Towards public fire. The tracks of my nature,
Subtly linking the crossing, were always lonely,
Unsponsored, misjudged, hardly Cornish at all.
Nowhere between Land's End and Tamar
Had a pen-stroke left a mark that guided my steps
Or cut a kindred passage.

Romantic sentiment - squires and halls,
Prudent ideals, academic precision -
What could these mean to me
Who needed the unschooled artist's crucible,
The revivalist's platform, the hermit's cell,
The theologian's tome open on granite, open to
    upland winds,
And the sex-mystic's pulse of moon-tokens on the
    loyal
Pressed lips and breasts? For almost half a century
I was so many selves in one skin
That the entangled contending veins
Would have snapped in early frost
Had I not found a unifying trust.

My character, like the scarred plateau
That bore me, had its geometry askew -
Lopped, slanted, swollen: the crystal peaks
Craned in a barren patchwork till, beyond art,
Outside the blood's moods and the mind's,
I found scope and motive in the far call
Rising through mother's and wife's prayer, breaking
    despair.

Louder than the sea that silenced Davidson,
Stronger than the poison that ended Lindsay's twang,
The old Damascus call brought me balance.
All my gifts straightened and tasted sweet
As the glib exhibit ceased to be the norm of advance
And the brooding ego the norm of retreat.

CHARLOTTE MEW

We tragic Mews - the Muse could only smirk
Like a cracked angel, tuning an artist fibre
In such a misbegotten brood.
I see that gabbling speck - my mother:
Four feet tall, her nerves in tatters,
Straining for gay defiance (the trick didn't work),
Fighting for breathing space among the normal.

Her fight was ours too; we knew the dwarf's terrors
In streets and rooms: shoulders thrusting above us,
Eyes glinting down with derision or pity.
Our questing minds were bent by the tiny bones,
Our passions choked and wrenched in midget frames:
No ascent to a wholesome clasp, a safe vista.
The blight soon broke my mother and Freda:
They were lodged in a madhouse. What of me, my
        claims?

Too sensitive - that's what got me split.
When the plane-trees were felled near my home
My heart bled - agony: I was robbed of communion
With a whole heaven of birds and leaves and soft
        shadows.
Then Willie died at ninety, chloroformed -
Our darling parrot who had mocked the men,
Making us laugh so, me and Anne.
But he couldn't grip his perch any more - he would lie
Suffering for hours in his cage, squawking feebly.
Just like me - too much like me
Since Anne went, since they buried her alive . . .

They did! They can't fool me: I told them all.
That's why I'm here in this rest-house for the mental.
While Dad lived he whisked us into illusion
At times, splashed money about, sent me abroad . . .
It's funny, but when I think of France,
Try to recall the Seine lights, the woods' grave solace,
Moon-flush like pure death on pungent harbours,
I see church stone, candles, an accusing glare
In the dusk where I played Madeleine.
I must have touched man's soul-plight, I suppose:
The poem I wrote was judged - well, blasphemous.
Priests would say I have paid the price
For my rebellion, my proud self-will. (What jargon
They use to abuse one's scorn of cant!)

But there were interweavings, flickers above the steel
Of my stoic code. I felt a presence
Spread around crucifix and saint,
A lift towards faith within my elfin body,
As if I might be convinced, grow normal and human
With a little more stretching. But the marvel snapped:
I was too small to hold it. I escaped.
Montmartre's bought women flashed. Earth, café
       meal . . .

It's *fin de fête* all right - a pretty *fête*!
I wonder if my friend guessed yesterday
Why I gave her that Hardy copy -
My poem he liked so much? She read the phrase:
'It's good-night at the door.'
Yes, I've locked the door.
Good-night, Anne. Good-night, Willie.

I'm outside the world. I found no grace:
The middle Cross falls like the plane-trees,
Sawn through by - what? Me? Sorry, God!
I can't sort it out, can't let the flickers tease,
Nor the spring air torment me at sixty.
The crushed little cat's last mew
(Still a Mew . . . oh, Christ!) will soon be silenced
While the March winds rattle on.

I've locked the door.
Good-night, Mr Hardy. You were very kind,
But you've been dead two months, so you won't mind.
They buried Anne alive, but I'll make sure
(Dear smirking Muse) there'll be no place
For doubt when they burst in, find the empty bottle,
And see the cold grimace under my white hair.

Charlotte Mew was a dwarf who wrote poetry, seeking in art a
compensation for her tragic remoteness from normal life. The at-
tempt failed and she killed herself in 1928.

CARADOC EVANS

The fighter had struck through fog,
Making a crusty art from the seethe of his Welsh blood,
Torn by Bible bones and capel flints
That jutted near the soft pagan witch-lore.
The sheep cowered from his spurting thunder;
He traced the infernal monologue
To the shepherd's mouth, mistaking, confusing,
Daemon-driven amid unctuous hints.
A crucifix and the collar of a dead dog
Were the same to him, symbols of suffering.

The crucifix is mute in his study;
Cader Idris, watchful as Sinai,
Leaves pillar and cloud opaque at capel Horeb,
Caradoc's fate unspelled. The grave slants high,
Rough and storm-pummelled; the slates rattle
Like his gnashing volleys. A battle-ebb,
Fall of a black wave is felt; the spittle
Of blasphemy is lost in a calm flood.

Where's the root of his twist?
In his lapses, his self-flagellation,
Despair drowned in drink? Or was it the rub
And the grind of the low strata, grounded ambition,
The disdain of rich gig-driving neighbours
For his widowed mother, his drapery job,
When he scribbled in quaint foreign English
On wrapping-paper - all these pressures denting
His peasant-proud, passion-heated base?

Naive as folk-tales, as terse and deadly,
Wales' wild son spurned the cultured grace,
Wrote raw and simple, and lived so, even in London.
He tasted chapel sermons there too,
Not believing, not worshipping,
Less wistful than Hardy in the pew,
Yet sometimes reverent, marking a Bible verse.

Does the satiric pew-haunting artist
Stand on pure rock-truth, hook the sham,
Expose it with hate terrific as a Christ-flash,
Or is the artist the fraud, the perverse flame,
The crafty vulture in the temple?
Caradoc's dust cannot answer.

The savage ironist has gone,
Leaving, amid his cruel fruit,
A few kind words for a nun or Methodist
The crucifix in his study is mute;
Cader Idris watchful as Calvary
See the farmers climb to capel Horeb.
The sheep must bleat around Brynawelon,
And his favourite hymn rise faintly through the mist.

Caradoc Evans was a Welsh novelist and story writer, bitterly at-
tacked for associating fantastic cruelty and sexual laxity with the
emotional fervour of the village chapels. He is said to have been a
sadist who projected and dramatized a deep-lying self-hatred.

GLADYS AYLWARD

Almost as small, and just as odd-looking
As any female genius or blue-stocking,
She was a finer medium, open to the straight flight
Of guiding whispers from the unseen, hooking,
Amid parlourmaid's chores, a destiny in limelight.

Cockney sparrow with the plain chirp and flutter,
Blundering and fogged at school - the rare shutter
Clicked for her cramped eyes, on the safe side:
Not where the ego dreams or the mystic would utter
Sleek wisdom, but where saints' rough facts abide.

Doggedly or with a child's smile beyond courage,
She dusted her way to a China passage;
Went alone, unfit, staking wildly like a poet,
But on God's prose level, a higher stage,
Where the stranger's cry for rescue is the magnet.

Fevers of the cultured scribbling spinster,
Goblin-damps of fancy, were matched in her
By reckless dartings among foreign hills
As the Voice prompted. Jap raids shook the preacher
While she crouched and yelled, knowing how the blood
    chills.

The month-long scramble across the mountains,
Leading the bombed-out horde, sleeping in dens;
The arrival, starving and weeping, at the Yellow River . . .
Then the dark spectre, drying identity . . . But Christ's
    rains
Came in rescue, not the suicide's quiver.

Gladys Aylward was a London domestic servant who, after being
rejected by missionary societies, went to China alone, guided by an
inner psychic awareness of God. She did a remarkable work of
spiritual leadership, suffering and recovering from a severe nervous
breakdown during the course of her activities. She became famous as
a subject for films and books.

VIRGINIA WOOLF REMEMBERS ST IVES

Above the huer's hut the clouds have no edges:
It's too near sundown, there's nothing left to grip.
All's floated loose, smudged in the sun's dyes,
In a soft padded riot: the clouds huddle together,
Wandering and woven and woebegone,
For us to look at before we scream.

When shape dissolves, the open trauma is on us,
Dismay, the brief laugh of hysteria,
Then the definite mesh, the icy pull through darkness . . .
I love Cornwall's unspoilt, unsparing candour,
Her seas so bold in cruel fantasy,
Her soil so pregnant with ancient terror.
I am drawn, I cry out and am touched
Too intimately, but my world was answered
From the first day I dreamed around St Ives.

Watch your mocking sea, dear huer - it's quite
        romantic!
I also am mocked and a mocker.
I can fancy your sad, tired scowl
In the cliff-top hut, probing the sundown flash
That is more reflection, mere empty water.
All through those weeks I spent at Talland House
The boats waited, the big nets were ready,
But your horn did not sound. You were honest:
You would not fool the simple fishers,
Nor mistake cloud-shadows for a shoal.

The mythical haul of pilchards!
A vast, gliding, phosphorescent shimmer
From millions of flicking fins,
Cold eager little bodies. Dense movement of life,
Gills breathing gently under the foam,
Goblin eyes rubbed by rocking currents,
Tiny mouths opening for marine food.
The whole delicate lovely thing could end
In the slimy mesh, the up-drag, the convulsive death;
But not at St Ives or Carbis Bay
During that loaded summer when I was ten.

The symbols grew confused: I am the huer,
And also the caught fish. I watch for a sea-breast glow
That means solid truth, but it does not come,
Though my father had worn a dog-collar
And blown his horn feebly, misreading the signs.
He reared me in silent guilt; I choked early
And shall die choking. But Cornwall soothes my fate:
Her images of cloud, wave, huer's hut
And lonely lighthouse (could the fish see that)
Pierced between dream and trauma, shaped something
(Though not hope), and my solid pages
Float out from a borderline.

Virginia Woolf, experimental novelist and critic, spent many
holidays in west Cornwall, and the Cornish landscape and seascape
helped to form her symbolism. After a vague religious phase she re-
lapsed into the agnosticism in which her father had reared her.

A CHOICE ABOUT ART

To Oswald Chambers

You went to the crag's edge with Van Gogh,
Saw the split gifts collide,
Bleeding their prophecies over the mountain-side.
As art student you plied the cunning brush;
As minister's son you itched for the rough
Rod of the preacher, the formless smiting rush.

On that night of struggle at Arthur's Seat
You followed Hopkins and bent,
Like him, your being to self-abandonment,
To years of beauty-mangling, dry grey soul-storms.
Man's sin, thick as Scottish sleet,
Froze your art's seed-bed and all creative charms.

Choice of the Kingdom Van Gogh had seen
But let slip for the sun's
Rank relish for colour - your Dunoon congregations
Soon found what it brought you: the uncanny power
That by-passed piety, showed the lean
Loll of self-indulgence, the Christ-thorn in flower.

Did you hear of Van Gogh's flight from Richmond,
His prayers frayed on a hussy,
The bullet-snap under a foreign tree?
The pulpit had lost a voice, the galleries gained
Some savage pictures. Fate must respond
To a man's choice, and your hammering voice
    remained.

But the setting changed and the cadence turned
In a marvel of restored tints.
From the cold sea-mist of Aberdeen, where the hints
Of faith and art first stirred you, the pattern moved
Past crag and thorn to the unspurned
Desert glamour, dawn-watches with your beloved.

At the Zeitoun base, near Cairo, the troops
You served were awed by the balm
Of your fertile marriage, gay amid camel and palm.
Your artist-nerves exulted, somehow redeemed:
A paradox barred to your old art groups,
Barred to Van Gogh, now bared its body and teemed.

Oswald Chambers, originally a painter, abandoned art for
evangelism and served for many years as a chaplain in Egypt. The
notes of his sermons were collected and published after his death,
and have had a phenomenal influence as guides to Protestant
devotion. Van Gogh made the opposite choice, abandoning
evangelism for art - with tragic consequences.

FRANCIS THOMPSON

Drab babble of the Thames somersaulted
Into rhythms of Aeschylus and Blake,
Whose work bulged the drop-out's pockets
At nightfall. His fugutive mind
Regarded the mixed myths with a drug-keyed stare:
Io-image of fate-stung humankind.
Incarnate in the child whore stumbling
Beer-fuddled from a gas-lit alley; Albion rising
Storm-cleansed among bloated tribes, calling for
    prophets.

The personal Hound who had driven this dreamer
From hospital odours to the higher wound
Pawed and breathed fiercely on the ragged refuge.
Francis lay, consecrating the Embankment
With a whispered prayer, a sick poet's assent.

Too far north to abate the fever,
His industrial cradle, Lancashire mills,
Fed him no solid ballast.
His litany spun towards opium sleep,
Wavered in purple haze: a tramp's feet, calloused,
Bore the weeping heart, the trance of rituals.

Fraternal hands roused him; his tottering steps
Found a path, a home door. A pure child's kiss of
    greeting
In gracious room snapped the doom,

Turning his sense-tracks innocent and young,
And the slow hallowed bell, the votive light,
Spelled bliss in the Hound's shadow
Where immortal lines were scrawled by his thawed
    fingers.

Io-image: was the guardian so immune
When the stage matured and the child's mother
    towered queenly?
Promethean fire somewhere, a hopeless passion
Raised to the ideal, stabbed and shyly vocal
Amid the slack shifts of the addict.
Struggle and flight and the Hound's shadow darker
On the two poets, the woman's proud prudent eyes
Reading and understanding the sacrifice,
Till the last flag of flame in Francis' body
Brought the nuns smiling, joyful in their unflawed
    secret,
To the still stone of Albion's weak, grace-harboured
    prophet.

Francis Thompson, Roman Catholic poet, was rescued from a down-and-out existence in London by his co-religionists, Wilfred and Alice Meynell, who encouraged and guided his erratic genius. He is best known as the author of 'The Hound of Heaven', but many of his poems show that his suppressed love for Mrs Meynell was sublimated in emotional attachments to her little daughters.

HOLMAN HUNT

Pre-Raphaelites! The self-styled priests
Of an unsullied splendour - the mediæval twilight
    gleam,
Arthurian magic, and the East's
Languor of mystic haze. We would redeem
England's soul once more, set the rich
Cleansing glow of colour on the drab wall,
Combat with knightly zeal the industrial itch,
Send heaven's ray obliquely, subtly
Against the Victorian smoke–pall.

Our aim was noble, our art-sense trained,
But a warp was in the hot blood:
The bright banner of the brotherhood
Was soon bedraggled, stained
With signs of madness and drunken splutter.
Beauty itself, its wild intoxications,
Blinded us to the snake's fang in the mist,
The brute-seed in the lofty rebel.

Jesus Christ's name headed the list
Of our exemplars. What an irony!
The hypocrisy of art! Some of our band
Kept mistresses, procured abortions,
Paid blackmail price for unseemly letters,
Or tasted divorce-court squalor. Millais and I
Were the least corrupted, I suppose.
But there were murky patches: my religious mission's
Dubious with daubs that wrung tears from Fanny
And sting Edith's pride now at my life's close.

That Egyptian brothel . . . though I had to climb
Those reeking stairs in search of a model.
The group awaited me, their backs to the door –
Veiled Moslem houris from the Nile slime
Or the desert. The veils rose and fell,
And I left hurriedly. Eastern violence!
Lewd faces gashed and bruised, some with teeth
        broken,
Not suiting my picture or my lust.
I was painting Christ, probing public conscience,
But I could not get morally focused.

The Arab chamber with its hot gaudy divans
Recalled the London web, the dusty amour:
Rossetti, Lizzie, West End courtesans –
And slum-bred Annie, wanton, easily bought.
I meant to marry her, not seeing the shame,
Nor caring, in her arms, what ideals I taught.
I paid for her schooling and she absconded
To live with wealthy rakes, then with Gabriel.

It's best forgotten. I preserved my fame,
Gave my virtuous wives prestige and travel.
Yet I am haunted. Serving a higher Power,
Misleading the pious. Annie twists the aim.
'The Light of the World' hangs crookedly,
Shaped in her impure flame.

Holman Hunt, Victorian painter of religious pictures, became
infatuated with a slum whore called Annie, and though in time he
made a respectable marriage, Annie's physical features remained on
many of his 'sacred' canvases.

ERIC GILL

His hand carved stone and cuffed Art,
So he worked with a clear conscience,
Serving the absolute Beauty, Augustine's vision,
Which breeds the polemic and the convert.
He was not split, but deeply unified
As craftsman and believer. With quiet joy
He chiselled the ritual image,
Humble as a monk doing penance
For his blind brethren who stumbled astray.

The taut fervid shadow of Whitefield
Had drawn grey angles over his hunger
As he sat, a neat boy, in the Brighton pew;
The affirming logic of Aquinas
Matured him among the Ditchling friars.
His spirit broadened through the incisive blend
Of credal cross-blades that high Art denied,
Making him function as a misfit,
Wary and chafing, his warm charity steeled,
Like a loyal saint's, on the ethic: what inspires,
And why, and who sets the limit.

Some said he fled from Art's inner circle,
Very well: let them say it. Gill's way is mine,
And it was Milton's (the pamphleteer
Blocking the poet for decades
Because the man must spread truth, fight for it,
Not just salute a Muse and rhyme a fancy).

Gill knew the lonely seizure
When trained technique guides the tool
To satisfy the pure sense of design;
But it was in faith's context, made meaningful
By priest's and preacher's motive - blasting idols,
Hurling the healthy norm at a sick culture.

Gill's discipline showed the only way
Of feeding and seeding the artist's throb
On the safe home's hearth. Outside this rule all's
    torment
Because all's ego: dark paths winding furtively
Back to the airs of the aesthetic snob,
The weird temples where sane bonds are shrivelled
At the heat of a whim, and the raffish prowlers,
Prostrated, obsessed by a private quirk,
Embrace their pointless martyrdom.

Bombs splintered church and salon as Gill died,
But what he served was unshaken.
Cathedral, Tube station and museum
Preserve the prayers he breathed in stone-work;
And there was the voice, sharp and urgent,
Sounding naive, pleading from simple pastures,
Talking of sacred arts unvexed by ambition,
Unwarped by misused genius - a world of proud
    workmen,
Singing in poverty. This ideal
Has dimmed, but a point of it was real -
The angle of grace, the Kingdom's revolution,
Starkly cut on our Mammon-ridden confusion.

27

A RENDERING

Finger-skill and blown breath on brass
Reach back to the penned notes of the composer,
Back to the germ of fire
That spread in harmonies of treble and bass,
Branching in light, kindling desire,
Now gathered in the mass.

The alert trained touch of the players
Fuses with a master's striving mood,
Interprets its tension and flow, confers
On the relaxed ear and spirit
The deep tongue struck by drum-beats of the blood,
Rolled from opaque turmoil, charged with it.

Did a haggard wife watch bitterly
As the notes first spilled, or a tavern wench
Smirk, having sown his black conflict?
We reap music from the stabbed ecstasy,
The smoky guilt, heaven's garret-crack, fate's
        wrench . . .
The band blares, rendering no verdict.

SALVAGED

I narrowly missed being born on a farm,
With all a rural poet's stock-in-trade
Brimming around me: cock-crow and calf-wail,
Plough churning, wain eased at the rick, milk-pail
And apple bough swinging at moonrise, rabbits shot.

But the tenant, my grandfather, died
Before my lungs breathed in my earthly lot.
My parents had to migrate: beds, chairs, tables,
The cumbrous dresser, a trunk full of books,
Were piled on a waggon, hauled past stables,
Up Goonvean lane under steely twists of cloud,
And along the flat bristly Slip
To a cramped cottage near a sand-tip.
Not yet born, I shared the upheaval
Only through my mother's grief and fears.

As a young schoolboy I scanned the farmhouse
With mild curiosity - then it vanished,
Swallowed by a clay-pit; and for thirty years
I saw the whole farm eaten away.
Dynamite, tip-waggons, scoops - they all combined
To rip and crush my parents' lost green world
Till not a post or grass-clump was left behind.

Was it this shock that pitched me so far
From the song of the pastoral poet?
Did I fear to love the sown soil, the blushing cluster,
Because I knew the white monster was potent,
Sure to obliterate beauty and make me suffer?

Perhaps so; but the intense need
To come to terms, reverse the process,
Make the wrecker seem not all malevolent,
Was strangely eased when I explored
The trunk-load of volumes carted from the farm.

Wet Sundays, the family shut indoors,
And I alone in the back bedroom,
Blessing the rain for making me secure
As I rummaged, kneeling amid piles
Of torn musty books – not a boy's usual diet.

They were chiefly grey Wesleyan or Puritan,
Akin to the Cornish ones at Haworth rectory;
But unlike prim Charlotte (who thought them mad),
I skimmed the foxed pages hungrily,
Finding clues that were to be shared
By a girl then in London, ransacking similar tomes.

Showing that the land's peace can deceive, seduce,
That thunder and flash and devastation
May mean that heaven is working on a soul,
Shifting the deep fixations, intending kindness.

PRIVATE POMPEII

To find my industrial Pompeii,
All in miniature, in subtle association,
I would turn from the main track, down a disused siding
That dropped in a snarl of vegetation
Under the high tip of the fissured, swollen
Dump at Trethosa, where past wrongs could sting.

That gravel wedge gripped in its ground belly
The house where my father had grown afraid,
And where, at the age of seven, I studied music,
But failed to learn it in such cramping shade.
Vesuvius in the ghostly bed
Rumbled louder than the organ,
And on the musty couch a violin
Always caught my eye, distracting
Before the moment of flight.

That cottage, where my pagan air
And discordant fingering were rooted, was gone from
     sight,
Beyond hope of excavation. What remained
Of my Pompeii myth was soon starkly seen:
Long rows of masonry, crumbling brick,
Pillars, fragments of wall, the tall
Broken columns of stacks. In sun-glare
The stone of the drying-sheds was marble-white,
But coarse and ill-smelling, close to the railway line.

I would push through thick reedy grass
On the derelict track, climb up some steps
To the level of the ruins and pass
Through a gap where a door once swung,
Then pad soundlessly over the broad kiln floor,
Which was inches deep in clay-dust. I would stoop,
Scraping harmless powder where, twenty years before,
Clay was baked as flames lunged and ran
Inside the furnace, under the kiln-pan.

My father had worked here, rammed his shovel
Into mica-mounds bare as icebergs and soft as dough,
And the wooden trolley had lurched to and fro
Between the open-air tank and the covered kiln.
No roof, not even a rafter still
Survived to help me picture
My father shrouded here, breathing hot steam
That fingered the discords of his dream.

But in my depths, even if mist clung
Around the ruins, I was aware
That my Pompeii fable would be outgrown -
Vesuvius, scorched bed, crushed roof and garden
Become a mere traveller's tale at my fate's turn,
And a sweet-stringed, post-pagan ardour be housed and
     born.

IN ROCHE CHURCH

Inland now, though soon to tread sea-sand again,
We kneel alone in the cool hill-top church,
Screened from Hensbarrow clay-smirch,
Guarded by clean pillars, free to marvel
At the way we ride the grey test, long past our vow.
Didn't the autumn winds howl warning
Of an ill-equipped and ill-timed venture in the wrong
Climate? Yet the calm tower
Is apt above our private gesture,
And the altar's mystery breathes through the centuries'
     dust
As her arm, eight years familiar, presses my waist.

There's a famous freak rock near us,
A black savage skull of a thing on the moor.
Monks built a chapel there and one wall stands
Facing the sea still, high on the schorl mass.
Gales from both coasts have struck the pinnacle
A thousand times, and shaken this church door
Which we approached under fragrant leafage
Up the lane from a July-scorched stile . . .
Something remains impregnable, holds evidence
Without a technique of defence.

Nimble cliff-climb up the crumbling stone stairs,
That we find true safety when storm knocks at night
Along our tissue of coast, swamping cave and landmark.
No: that's the cunning animal dodge,
Not for monks or the deeply married.
We must show man's stature, massive as the floundering
     assault;

We must cease to sharpen our wits
In training for trivial exits.

Man's way - our way at least - is a faith trandescent,
Hammered by storms from birth, clumsily sculptured,
Often seeming an obtuse image,
Neither skilled nor frantic when the boat splits
Or the tide traps, yet always preserved.
Nobody knows how. We are too intent
On the unseen touch, angel's wing, communion with a
    soul-mate,
To care whether our rescued feet
Tread sand or rock or moorland spur
Or the paved church. A random whim
Of unforced reverence has made us kneel,
Heads bowed, awed by our love's survival.

DROUGHT ON A CLAY RIDGE

The slopes look drained and old, passive as Egypt,
Though the hot pyramids are white mineral waste
And the insects are still English.
A freak tropic climate has been testing
The wrong fibres and the wrong blood: all's in collapse.
Tired worried eyes watch a mummified landscape,
The natural bits of it gone brown or yellowish
Long before autumn. Not a shoot of pure green
Breathes on the baked clods or between the dazed stones.

I can't recognise my own garden hedge:
It's all straw - or more like a heap of shavings,
Crisp, loosely packed, unlike a rooted substance,
Unlike normal grass in winter.
Nothing here has had its day:
Wizard weather brought wizened stillbirths;
The sap's leap was stunned by the rainless grin overhead.

I loved to tilt the strong foxglove cups,
So sleek amid the rough leaves, here in summer.
But this year they did not open:
Small deformed skins tried to thicken,
But were scorched dry, shrunk like tissue-paper
And dropped in shreds from dead, rigid stems.

Almost daily, in lanes that sweat tar,
A fire-engine clangs and rattles through dust-clouds,
Through odours from over-heated walls and wood,
Racing to a field or down-patch
Where something that should drip sap is ablaze.

The smoke does not rise or spread fast
In the compressed atmosphere:
It huddles and thins around the absurd commotion
Till the weary, exasperated firemen
Are back on the road again, heading for more trouble
From the bland incendiary sun,
Leaving another black sore where the soot's
A shameful substitute for bloom and berry.

Weird and desolate in a new way
Are the mine-scarred hills, the pyramid-shadowed
     valleys:
The native feels himself a foreigner
When the climate disregards his roots.

COPPICE TARN

The old coppice tarn – were it still here,
I could expunge or exorcise the cringe of fear
Which made my child eyes dilate in that hollow.
Under a grown love-spell now, I could scan,
Curious and immune,
The witches' den's dark Sabbath of sagging elder,
Elm, nettle-tooth, puffed thumb of toadstool,
Curdled green slime on the slow,
Rarely ruffled eye of veiled water.

We would come in over a high tight bank
Which fed a scrawl of thickets to the brink
Of the cliff that dropped brokenly to the pool;
Then, squeezed close, heads cautiously bent,
We would tread the slant
Of a path that curved down between brake and boulders
Almost to the tarn's surface level.
So weird there, cramped in the tree-shrouded hole,
With stabbing glints caught through reed and furze.

A rotten fence at the coppice tail
Would have given us exit to fields and the hand-rail
Plank bridge across the stream. Good to get clear,
You would agree, of that eerie spot
Where my favourite cat
Was drowned by a ragged old village man
While I watched and shivered . . . Well,
It's all lost in clay-waste now – nothing here
But white dumps and tanks: no pool-green or tree-green.

HENRY MARTYN

(1781-1812)

Deaden the fire. Why did the Moslems lay me
In this furnace of an inn, on the mud floor?
No air: each breath is agony,
The sweat pours, heat makes the winds shrill
Through my feverish brain, like the howling,
Weird and heathen, in the mountain passes.

I swooned on mule-back under the sting
Of the Himalayan blasts, was sick, delirious.
The nightmare journey from India
Ends here. It's Tokat, isn't it, this place
Where the plague rages? I'll die soon,
An unknown chaplain, eased by no friendly face
Or kind word, in the wilds of Persia.
I hoped to reach Cornwall, marry Lydia,
Though I still questioned . . . Deaden the fire

How long did she stay on Marazion sands,
Or watch through a casement, that August day
When the *Union* - that troopship of Nelson's fleet -
Limped crossly along Mount's Bay?
I stood on deck, and all England's
Gifts to me seemed burnt away
With the sun on the shrivelling Mount.
Now my fever mounts and I shrivel,
Knowing that was my last home-touch: my Truro
     street
Lost, and my classic Cambridge fount.

She would promise nothing, though her Celtic eyes
Showed a love we both feared – a tremulous passion
Matching mine and fought, as mine was,
In defence of faith's higher claims.
A staunch Dissenter, she prayed with the sick,
Had pious qualms . . . Were we, as our friends said,
Misled, morbidly ascetic?

I am not sure, for I have seen
What the absence of such strife can mean:
Lust defied, the monstrous idol brooding,
Smeared foreheads rubbing the ground;
And then the death-will . . .
I came too late once: the widow had leapt on the pyre,
Her ashes joining her husband's, by the Ganges.
The ritual custom, horror . . . Deaden the fire.

I cried aloud against pagan darkness;
I preached to the whores at Calcutta,
Mistresses of our troops. No seed took root:
They were too brutish, alive only for male power,
Sensual submission – kicks or the coarse caress.

Had Lydia shared my work, a reverent bride,
Would they have caught a spark, a ray of desire
Which my pale celibacy denied?
Useless to ask. Our sacrifice, if folly,
Is final now, awaiting heaven's verdict,
As my new translation awaits the Shah's.
That's one gain – my Persian scripture . . . How will
    she learn
I am in my grave? St Michael . . . Deaden the fire.

Henry Martyn, born at Truro, gave up a brilliant university career as
a classical scholar and became a pioneer missionart in India. He
translated the Bible into various Indian languages and finally into
Persian. His short life was complicated by his unfulfilled love for a
Cornish girl, and he died while on his way back to England, where
he hoped to resume their romance.

LA SALETTE

Altitude too high,
   Roots crazily vain:
Under conniving glaciers
   The false tints preen.

Shallow gorge breeds tension;
   Mountain pastures are too harsh:
The horned beasts obey blindly,
   Driven to the gully's marsh.

Then the two herders sleep
   In the magnetic sun:
Too young to make love,
   But touched for an explosion.

They awake in panic
   Over wandering brute-life:
Primitive, Catholic
   Child minds act the grief.

A terrible radiance
   Floods the autumn scene:
Figure and voice transfix
   Melanie, Maximin.

They see, in the woman's tears,
   Cosmic peril absolute:
Every glacier wounded,
   Every petal shut.

It's the dark human projection
   Stirring the divine storm.
Ironic choice – these urchins
   Must grasp and affirm.

The cows feed unwitting;
   Child tongues soon babble the news:
'The blessed saint was weeping.'
   Rude fibre shuns the vows.

The pair strut from the gorge-trance,
   Stumble to slipshod years:
If heaven opened, the vision
   Fails in their folly's course.

Shiftless, evasive sparks
   Grimace at the cloisters;
Cunning thrives on the thronged road;
   Shrill Alpine ego blusters.

Pilgrims' tapers burn steadily
   To a love veiled and sorrowing,
Yet striving to connect, convey,
   Restore joy – sometimes succeeding.

The alleged appearance of the Virgin Mary to two children on a mountain at La Salette in 1846, and the strange experience, referred to in the following poem, of John Diego, the Mexican Indian whose tribal cloak or tilma, bore the supposed miraculous imprint of the Virgin, have been much discussed in recent years.

JUAN DIEGO

(1474–1548)

Morning Mass would make me forget the desert,
Even the heart's desert, cold bed, my squaw
Gone under sand, away from cactus, totem,
And the strange Spanish faces we used to hate.
I started out, racing wild as a mountain lion,
To receive the white God, to celebrate
Under His birth-moon – I, the Indian convert,
Poor Juan, the despised Franciscan.

A dark red hand above me had dissolved:
Aztec mother-goddess, cruel weaver,
Leaving the coarse *tilma* blank of meaning,
And the bare body more blank, meaning only lust.
I felt her melt in the candle-flame
My white brothers lit: our Mexican dust,
Our feathered serpent, no longer shuffled
Glinting in my blood's bowed dream.

But my altar, at that December daybreak,
Was not in the village church. I was chosen,
They tell me, as heaven's messenger.
I was certainly stopped at Tepenac hill,
First by bird-choirs, then a young girl's voice
Piercing down from the rocks where our pagan
        temple
Mouldered in ruins. I climbed, wide awake,
Through frost-veils to our new Mother. I still rejoice

That I saw and heard and lived, with the sky's
Queen breathing on me, calling me 'little son,'
Bidding me tell the bishop: 'Raise a chapel
To the true Light on Tepenac.' I ran,
Marvelling and exultant, through the barren glare
Of wintry sunrise, found the holy man
In his palace. He could sympathise,
But needed miraculous proofs. I was troubled there.

Back at the sacred hill she was waiting,
And all the rocks were fragrant with miracle roses.
She folded a few in my *tilma* . . . lovely hands,
Such tender skill, as shown once among oxen.
And then, at the palace, the discovered imprint,
Her image on my *tilma*. How often
Will men look with awe, kneel before it, the coarse
     plaiting
Aglow with colour, her pure face and all it meant?

AT HARDY'S BIRTHPLACE

All is Quaker-simple here, firm and remote,
With the heavy strength of old iron and timber,
Except for the lean wooden rail
Flanking the frail
Stunted stairs. The upper room where he wrote
Breathes a hard sincerity, like his birth-chamber.

You can't polish thatch or fashion elegance
From anything here at Bockhampton:
The brawl of wood and heath
Threw a shaggy sheath
Around the boy's steps, the cider-warmed dance,
And the shams his mature mind stamped on.

No break-through from these wilds to sophistication,
However long he might brood and search.
At the lattice he watched owls glide,
And the blind moon ride
In irrational scorn or sly elation,
To grope for the death's-head in Stinsford church.

All created things groped down to a mocking mouth,
With a sturdy hearth the brief antidote:
Love's jest by the friendly fire
Need not enquire
How far the wind has veered from south,
Why the rabbit cowers, frozen by snake or stoat.

His sceptic tools were sharpened on the edge
Of briar and nettle, not the slick
Poison of the urbane flash
Amid cigar ash
In the distinguished salons. His pledge
To honest thought was homespun and authentic.

These beams press low, yet the rooms seem airy
 enough,
Glowing and warm near his June birthday.
If a pitying sadness springs
For the stumbles and stings
He was doomed to, there is holier stuff
In the pervading aura - no dank decay.

The death's-head gloats in the church and the heart
 moulders,
And Max Gate hides some dingy scars;
But a plain perception strove
Through his clotted grove.
He wrenched a cosmic woe to his shoulders:
Now his threshold creaks cheerfully; a plump thrush
 hovers.

Hardy's old church at Stinsford contains a macabre 'death's-head'
monument, erected in 1723 by Lora Grey, Lady of Kingston Maur-
ward manor, as a reminder that her parents were skeletons!
 Max Gate was the scene of much domestic discord: neither
Hardy's first wife, Emma Gifford, nor his second, Florence Dug-
dale, could finalize his search for the ideal woman.

DIETRICH BONHOEFFER

Crooked cross on the muffed, tolled acre
Told death's reign in iron, barbed wire,
Bullet and crematoria smoke.
Buchenwald of ill fame (faded
After thirty years' post-Nazi slime, the shame
Of man's coming of age) displayed its back-drag
Into primeval nurseries. Bully and victim
Naked as in their first, fenced twilight: robe or rag
Of reason was torn, leaving snarl and slobber.
Even the faith-tongued, wilting amid vermin,
Felt the rosary rot while the gallows hemp stayed
     strong,
And the slammed hypothesis of a loving Maker
Echoed mockingly through the gurgling skein.

The young pastor with the poet's eyes
Kept his secret, musing calmly apart,
Tracing transcendence in the base day's dole.
Thoughts wrung from Hegel, Goethe, Barth
Flocked with clear peace of the Danube summer,
Bavarian forests in the free years, and warmer ties
Edging to poignancy: the girl he would never wed
Vanishing from the cell door at Tegel . . .

The true Cross turned crooked under pressure:
His lovely trust and prayers knotted confusedly
With the cool brain's warp. Blind guesses would
     stumble
Beyond the camp barrier, touching religionless man,

Who seemed spilled, drained of creed-props, over
        broken countries,
Shrugging at gutted churches. The captive pastor
Saw a Cross that meant mere crumpled deity,
A heaven that knew only secular service
From the adult nature's autonomy.

The camp gates opened in savage rain
For Bonhoeffer's final journey.
The truck rattled on beside the stung Danube
Under trees that did not rattle: the month was April,
With hushed knots of leaves and buds passively
        bowing.
And he knelt at Flossenburg, the last plank straight
        again
To his acquitted faith. An infinite mercy,
Moving above death-cell and execution yard,
Annulled for him the blind probe
And the secular tolling.

Dietrich Bonhoeffer, German theologian, was imprisoned and
executed for his involvement in a plot to assassinate Hitler. The letters, prayers and other religious writings which he composed in cap-
tivity have become spiritual classics.

JIM ELLIOT

Rugged wrestler, Wheaton-trained, tough as Hemingway,
He saw life stripped and God-raided;
His look was gay or thunder-shaded
As the beckoning hibiscus by the Curaray.

He tore himself loose from culture; a sinewy flame
Lit his raw track to the Absolute.
Truth peeled was truth beyond dispute:
He hacked through convention to the bare cloven Name.

Religionless faith, more radical than Bonhoeffer's,
Blazed its challenge through his hard grip:
Unmoved amid civilised worship,
He strained for a fall where the wild tangle suffers.

The single outer Word, printed or prayer-caught,
Guided and sealed stubbornly
Decisions that gave sheer agony
To his male roots when storming nature brought

Thrust of love's bloom and the Voice said 'Sacrifice'.
He scorned the pseudo-mystic stuff:
'The secular is sacred enough;
The God within must bid the sweet sap rise.'

He cried: 'I'm mad for her, God, but I'll obey
Your opening call from a mud floor
In the sweating jungle of Ecuador.'
Yet he was no monk, sailing south with this price to pay.

Five years of abstinence, unappeased desire,
Witness to omnipotent law,
Objective mandate checking his flaw
Of self-fulfilment: still he prayed for her.

The test-ground was stark and lurid: frenzy of bull-fights,
River floods, danger from boa, puma,
Mosquito: he fought malaria,
Heard Indians scream, drowning or dying of snake-bites.

The will, the principle, never the personal instinct,
Based his sure steps till he saw truth's dawn
Change Quichua faces as love shone
In dark tribal eyes; then the denied dream linked

With the ripe phase of the mandate. Orchid and
        coffee-palm
Brushed the beloved: she was at his hut,
At the crest of her Kingdom vision that shut
For so long the earth-pulse from the spirit's psalm.

Their sanctions, as rebel pioneers, allowed
No room for a churchy marriage service:
God and a drab old Quito office
Rebuked the hollow shows. And when Elliot bowed

On the Curaray airstrip, pierced by the lance of an Auca,
Martyred for making Christ his chief,
A twin faith rebuked the clouding grief
In the woman clasping his child at Shandia.

Jim Elliot, a rebel American missionary, was murdered in Ecuador
in 1956.

51

THE RESTORED SEE

When foreign sails wagged on bowing masts,
Bringing the first Christian tongues to Cornwall,
Fal and Lynher plunged their wet blades,
From springs on the unsheathed haggard moor,
Through the heavy robes of forests.
The dyed tribes hunted, fought, used ritual
That clung to earth-roots, bore the slime of nets,
Or the knife's tongue that spoke of blood, blessed
By Druid wisdom when full moon at midnight
Coupled the cowled poles of lust.

The gaunt saints landed, banded
Boldly on the banks of Lynher and Fal.
Cell and chapel rites were ordered,
Stormed pagan pride with love-toned song and prayer.
Fountaining truth rinsed, here and there,
A local ruler free of the low lore,
Till royal gates received a flushed prelate.

Look back now, probe closely
Into that embryonic twilight.
What was the movement, heading
Towards the rebirth we celebrate?
An advance in religious apprehension?
Rome's root of culture shading us with a long branch
That thickened to papal tyranny,
Clotted with the carnal mitre?

There were abuses, but the sure succession
Pressed on through warped cycles, checked the
     invader,
Survived castle-crash, forest-cut, the expansion of
     mines
In Cornish soil and general human knowledge:
Christ's Body wove the Triune Light's designs.

Around the marshy Lynher
Germanus was heard of and honoured:
The Pelagian growth was hacked hard
Till sound fruit gleamed in Cornwall's first see,
Crowning us within the spirit's homeland.

The shepherd's staff flashed briefly
West of the Tamar, then withdrew,
Thinning to Exeter: priest and friar
Stumbled through mist, slipped on sand,
Waiting and wasting in the medieval ebb.

A new slant of light followed their burial:
Fierce Fox, intrepid Wesley,
Claimed and reaped here, seeing no bishop's palace,
No episcopal spires reflected
On our pulsing rivers, but feeling faith's pulse
In the unsheathed, unjewelled Word.

Clay was found: with the last change,
The industrial age, the tongue of science,

Came the queenly gesture: Peter's key,
In Cornish diocesan grace again,
Unlocked fresh splendours by the Kenwyn,
Dragging no gargoyle smirk

From the distorted past. The carved stone soared
High above shops, warehouses, squat church towers,
Bridges and raw back-streets caught in the dense
Dip of hills north of the Fal's fork.

Satellite at St Germans, the revived orb,
Rules ripe after leanness and burning,
While the Truro crest peals unscathed
With a century's tides and weathers flung and spent.
Cathedral chimes greet the foreign flags
That wag on quay-moored masts:
The Christian tongue is clear on the modern current.

The Truro Anglican diocese was established in 1877, many years before the cathedral was finished.

54

IN A TRURO GARDEN

To Margaret Shirley

A summer hour of infinite scope,
Pulse and patchwork restful – path, mown slope,
Hot slant on neck, brow, right cheek or left
As I turn at her supple urge,
Then tunnel-feeling, eclipse, cool draught,
Stiff boughs scraping till we emerge.

We stoop at a sleepy pool's rim,
Touch wet stone – I fancy the gleam
Quiver, get quenched by cloud-shifts;
Then it's flower-shapes at my finger-ends –
Winged, grooved or studded: a petal lifts,
Rough and spongy, a smooth tip bends.

Now, higher up, we're in the orchard:
Pleasant to feel my forehead
Nudged by a living apple,
A fruit still fed among leaves,
In sight of the slim clear grey cathedral
Which answers the bad fruit – Eve's.

It's a spreading answer, we can tell:
The vines thrive here on the wall;
There's an unclogged scent, a sunning cat –
No scare from a serpent's hiss,
No sylvan treason. Across the flat
Flushed tongue of our city the spires spill bliss.

This poem describes a visit my wife and I paid to the home and
old-world garden of Mrs Shirley at Vean, near Truro Cathedral, in
the 1970s.

WEYMOUTH

For Naomi, Sharon, Jonathan and Paul

The two sad shadows - George the Third
And Hardy the second - have conferred
A calm depth on the friendly town.
A poignant dignity, no menace,
Moves me on the bridge, the sands, going down
Some avenue or garden terrace,
Tapping a mooring-post, an ancient house-face.

The White Horse gleams above Osmington,
Neither leprous nor ghostly: crisp chalk and sun,
Sane and sturdy, meet there, and the bay
Rides royal with steamers and yachts.
The sick king stared at the sulphur spray,
And the poet sighed over fate's black plots,
But I sense the purged scene, the smiling mascots.

Shingle and mist weave no morbid spell
Between Wyke and Upwey wishing-well.
If a raven croaked on the crumbling cliff-fort,
I would heed only the laughing children
Who trust the song-bird, the poet unhurt.
Fate's dark dice drowns here, a bright ball is thrown,
Caught, like my kingdom, from love alone.

BETHEL

A bleak spot was chosen, where narrow lanes twisted
Irritably down to a stream and narrow lives
Twisted irritably down to death's river.
'Build here,' said the guides, 'a chapel
Whose straight, spurred walls will curb the crooked ways.'
The surrounding plough-scars sang their parable:
Soon the good seed flashed from its solemn cover,
The cramped valley had its fold of praise.

Beyond living memory, the rustic tongues,
Above long beards and frock-coats, poured the pure grain,
In Victorian sunshine or smoky lamp-rays,
Over the full pews, over veils and bonnets,
Mouldy muffs, ragged shawls, and men's caps,
Smelling of hayricks or kiln-fumes, shoved under the
        boards.

'Come, O Thou Traveller unknown . . .'
Hurl of Wesley's words
In a smouldering bay of Celtic voices.
Rasp of interior discords
Left by the crackling sermon: each soul alone,
Wrenched at a raw Jabbok. Twist of a Hand shaping
The straight, spurred lives, soon proved by the daily trade.
Preachers and flock on their farms and sand-tips,
Housewives at wash-tubs, made the choices
Which checked the casual slant, the running clay-bed.

Music behind the bitter crossroads,
Plucked from those organ-keys, drew the dale to culture:
Handel and Bach matched the naive ripple
And the hoarse drive of iron wheel and coulter.
Classic touch, trained choirs, followed the reapers' track
After the uncouth grapple.
Under the same grey roof, rough dialect
And elegant cadence bore the straight, spurred glory.

Roots of my story quiver
Around that bare Trethosa Bethel.
My bubbly, field-toughened grandfather
Clapped and shouted in the pulpit,
And a grave-toned minister
Sprinkled the christening drops on my face
As my infant eyes blinked at the communion rail;
And there, fifty odd years later,
I spoke vows at the end of a twisted lane
When I entered, bride-blessed, the straight, spurred union.

War-planes have crossed the dale,
Sparing the stubborn roof, though creeping apathy
Drained the pews, closed the gallery.
Time ripens, time bereaves,
But I rejoice with the Traveller
Whose plough-scars nurtured, too, my rebel sheaves.

ISLE OF SLINGERS

Tension and wind-torn rhythms: this is no place
For a glib rhymer, but I celebrate
The awesome cacophony of a twisted islet:
I sprang, myself, from an odd, constricted race.

While convicts split the blinding stone
And a girl's skull grins in the museum,
I strain through the whole choric poem
Of crime and cave-heat, dignity of clan.

East, west and south the ever-craving
Sea: no space to spin a pastoral line.
Arrows sang from the scored walls of Rufus: rain
Kindled the unfenced beds at bride-proving.

Weird as Penwith in some weathers, more stark and
    cramped,
Yet bearing Roman culture, Latin blood,
The wedge of rock on which King Charles hid
And Hardy brooded, slings me a note: 'Exempt.'

Cromwell found his man and Hardy
Never found his woman; yet, coming here
With traces of Cromwell's creed, I found a clear
Echo of the heart's glad discovery.

I trod with my well-beloved the uneven floor
Of Avice's Cottage - tiny as a cell.
We pictured the helicopters, modern and cool,
Darting above, and motor-boats tense by the shore.

Their throbbing chimed with our theme – release and
    rescue,
Wing and winnowing that snap the huddled spell.
Classic or brutish, the flat past juts: the coil
Of chafing mystery is loved in a broad view.

MAPPOWDER REVISITED

To Gerard Casey

The old Powys lodge is barred to us:
Fable and litany have gone from it
Since I alighted, young, warm from a dusty car,
And met the hermit at the lounge window. I touch it now,
Gravely, knowing he died here, calm in a russet-leaf fall,
Rebuking our century.

I could see behind him the arched doorway,
Slightly blurred but accessible to me
Even without guidance. My inward eye,
Which had borne so much Venus-white pit-glare,
Welcomed the portal dusk, the rich bursting land.

Intense rural smells are still the same -
Horses, thatch, the immoderate summer perfume
Of banqueting trees and flowers . . .
There was a feast, a crest of prevision,
A veil rent amid the mixed odours.
I had long cherished, from a different angle,
His picture of a God, who was not Pan,
Moving among the virgins.

In this hour of vindication,
When the lodge is too bitter-sweet,
We pass on to the churchyard,
Small and mellow, just a few steps up the lane.

I bend over the Powys tombstone:
Smooth curve of the carved book,
Rough inscription, meaning only a marriage
And two deaths.

We are reverent, feeling the pulse
Of a marriage and two lives;
And for us, as for that strange hermit,
The heart is in the pew, the cool humble station
Which means listening and communion
Till a sunshaft finds the golden Cross.
Gaze on the mystery, as he gazed
After his pen dried, and you have the clue
To my presence again in Dorset.

I would not return with the gleam unfulfilled,
For a poet's debauch of nostalgia and lamentation.
Sitting beside my partner in Powys' pew,
I share the great silence
Of earth at evening and heaven timeless - both totally real.

T. F. Powys, novelist, and story writer, abandoned literature for a life of mystic meditation and retired to the rectory lodge at Mappowder, Dorset, in 1940. I visited him there in 1950, and in 1978 my wife and I stood at his grave in Mappowder churchyard.

SANDSFOOT CASTLE GARDENS

Damp-haired in the stone memorial shelter,
We sit while a shower veils Portland harbour
And the palms look strange, marking no oasis,
Rejecting the desert image, since their fruits,
Like the buds of the neighbouring rose-bowers, swell
Between the cove and surburban Rodwell.

Along the railings of the Tudor castle,
Now a ruined fort, the new drops run,
Abreast of today's history –
Our history even, freed from siege and dungeon
And the monastic relics filched, misplaced
When our royal goal could not be traced.

Soft Channel rain glides, too, from the slim green
        banners
Hoisted by sap on the live ringed pillars,
The palm trunks. You watch the leaves dance,
While I recall white crystals and the red
Fanatic tinge on humped hills on dawn broke,
Etching a scraggy thorn-clump. How different here,
        instead,
Is the push of the delicate palm-roots,
Strong and confident through dense English earth,
With no shift and cackle of dry grains,
No whirlwind on a scorching horizon.

Outside, near the steps, the naked sundial
Has ceased to show the hour: it's a graven stump,
But not a silent sphinx. It was warm with sun
When we passed it, and it spoke,
Not of time but the unshadowed smile.

I have questioned often, questioned the worth
Of the long pain and mirage, the rotten clay-fields,
Or the cruel fate distorting clay-fields and me.
I hardly care where the blame goes:
Five pattering minutes more
And we shall caress together
The laughing tongue of the palm tree,
The damp full lip of the rose.

CHESIL BEACH

My feet tread the fragmented crust,
Slipping between enormous pebbles massed
In salty dyke-piles above the checked flow
That crawls and cranes through crannies, its Channel-
    powered jabs
Dislodging some lower slabs
With a dull submerged rattle. The miles-long heap
Has no angles or splinters: the pebbles, fawn or grey,
Shine smooth, rounded like eggs, stacked in shrill
    profusion
Near the dignified west curve of Weymouth Bay.

I am no foreigner here
If one can judge by an atmosphere.
This is my birth-image - freak and chaos,
A stammer of stone where custom called for sand,
The hard proud lump where you'd expect glued grains
Meek in a flat dough of convention.
A wilful breach of geological rules
Is pleasing to one who has evaded schools,
Sought the rare pattern, the fantastic stress,
The awkward blessing on the soul's isthmus.

I do not lurch on these stones alone:
She who gaily slithers beside me
Has long observed the tide's strange focus
And drawn comfort from seeing it barred
Where the tarred causeway, the quick friendly
    headlights,
Relieve the dusk-harsh gabble and rinsing.

We're on the Portland side - the Isle of Slingers
With its high-walled, efficient jail.
A tide has entered there, made some stones ring:
We were privileged guests with the singers,
The guitar-throb in the prison chapel
Where the convicts are rounded. Freak and chaos
Were the criminals' heritage and mine,
Since we were not of docile grain;
Only, for some reason, I am free
To come back here, taste human love's vivacity
And innocently scramble
From primeval pebbles to the brisk normal road.

EILIDH BOADELLA

Night sky as Keats saw it
Over the Lulworth, but here the shore
Is a mass of clanking loose-jointed armour,
With the dark sea springing to claw it.
The girl sits on a restless, faintly rattling ridge,
Dim in starshine, her waist-length hair
Tugged and tossed like her invaded spirit.

The waves whisper, 'Millions of children starve';
The pebbles rasp, 'Some children have abortion:
They didn't stay starved long enough,
And they forgot the pill.'
Cruel confusion, a world's woe breaking in
Too soon on the tender nerve.
She murmurs, 'I must empty myself, I must serve.'

Her poet-fibre withstands
Briefly, clinging to beauty.
'Bright star, enchant my Dorset still . . .
No, I am beyond, I am dedicated.
Bright star, would I were constant as
Mother Teresa's helpers in Calcutta.

'The foul streets sweat, the creeping shadows are
        callous.
Lift the dustbin lid: there's a baby inside,
Its brown skin smelling of scabs.
We'll snatch and rescue . . . My hands
Must do more than stroke these Chesil slabs:
So few get the vision - so few.'

Abottsbury holds some African trees
In its tropical gardens, up there on the hill.
'Black children are dying in famines, massacres:
I feel these smooth stones turn to splinters
Of human bones. My head has shed
Dream-ground that spilled glib rhymes
Over flowers' tints and birds' trilling.
How can these self-fulfilling
Poets live with their conscience?
I must answer the wider homecall.

'Bright star, Lulworth way,
Good-bye! Brighter star,
Bethelehem way, empty me of all.'

Eilidh Boadella was a young Dorset poet whose verse was published posthumously in *I Won't Paint any Tears* (Outposts, 1981). She had a profound religious experience which made her choose a life of poverty and sacrifice. She died in a fire at a London Mother Teresa hostel in March 1980.

FLORENCE BARCLAY

Jersey-born balm-bringer first breathing holiday air
By mistake, it would seem, or by a nudge
Of whimsical heaven: her embarrassed parents,
Returning from France, had expected the birth at home,
At Limpsfield rectory, among the Surrey hills.
The truant light in the brown baby eyes
Blessed the random isle and was soon sheltered
In a clerical garden, in the broad-brimmed family prayers.

There was no false step in her quest:
It was scarcely a quest, but rather a joyous racing
To embrace the visible mercies, multiplied
Till the music soared and the charged, magnetic hands
Fed and soothed a host of thin, scarred souls
Who misread life as drift and bafflement,
Cloyed dreams and grim endurance
Of satires that sharpened religious doubt.

Her honeymoon burned amid Christ's palms:
Her parson-husband knew his Palestine,
And knew his bride and she conceived
In the holy East and bore a child at nineteen.
Through forty years of sunshine
She was creative in the exempt ideal:
She never gave a kiss that staled,
And never sowed a book in the grudging desert.

She would sit, writing with an easy smile
And a bubbling heart, high up in the snows of St Moritz,
Or with a more serious exultancy
In the English graveyard near the Arno,
Beside the tomb marked simply: 'E. B. B.'
She caught the psychic tongue of Casa Guidi,
And mediated the poets' towering love
That chimed with her own bliss.

Relief and rebuke, this gracious pattern,
To us whose youth was all purgatory,
With the tusked, moon-bleared surmise ·
That bearers of profound truth
Must suffer the drive along the stormed road,
Finding and giving no pleasure,
Crying hoarsely of new light
Out of their endless woundings.

I reaffirm now what Florence felt
Among her Browning relics and at Wimpole Street,
Where I touched the carved stone and iron she fingered,
And my wife's warm hand unbolted the full depth.

Florence Barclay was a best-selling novelist of the early twentieth
century. She was deeply influenced by the Brownings, but shunned
literary society. She avoided all tragic and sordid themes, drawing
her inspiration from her serene happiness as a vicar's wife.

FILMING AT GUNHEATH

For, Kate, Zoe and Cerris

Trim but empty, the cottage is doomed,
Down by the working jaw of the pit,
In the path of the poised rubble;
The wide green gate and the shaggy fruit-trees
Soothed by the unsuspecting sun.

A brief reprieve, for my sake,
Has made the shell a hive, a stage.
Carpenters hammered up false walls;
Quaint furniture was fixed, old faded pictures,
Cracked and musty gear, to frame my past.

I touch coarse matting, a rusty Cornish range,
A battered organ and antique bedposts:
There's a dog, like my dead one miles away.
Actors and actresses, garbed as my family ghosts,
Lift the roots of my lost nightmare.

Within this house, before the walls crumble,
A small blind boy will whimper on the stairs,
A shabby youth rush from a tear-tapped typewriter
Into scourging silence, sobbing a barbed name;
A mother will weep at her prayers.

But the screened and budding schoolgirls
Who play the brighter roles, confirm my safety.
I am here as a married visitor,
A man of few questions. Let others ask
Why the pain had to be: I merely bless each mask.